SURVIVING PASSAGES

SURVIVING
PASSAGES

ANDREW GREIG

Illustrated by
James Hutcheson

Canongate 1982

First published in 1982 by **Canongate Publishing Limited,
17 Jeffrey Street, Edinburgh, Scotland**

© 1982 Andrew Greig

© Illustrations 1982 James Hutcheson
to Robin Williamson

ISBN 0 86241 025 8 hardback

ISBN 0 86241 026 6 paperback

The publishers acknowledge the financial assistance
of the Scottish Arts Council in the publication of
this volume.

Typeset by Hewer Text Composition Services.
Printed in Scotland by Summerhall Press Ltd., Edinburgh.

For the Visitors

Some of these poems have previously appeared in: *Akros,*
Aquarius, Bananas, Cencrastus, The Fiddlehead (Canada),
The Honest Ulsterman, Lines Review, The New Edinburgh Review,
The Poetry Review, Rune (Canada), *The Scotsman,*
The Scottish Review, Stand, Quarto.

1

2

3

ONE

A WORD OF WARNING/FORWARD!

Poet, could you put your song
into ma ear
a wee bit less perversely?
You made my brain buzz
like a faulty striplight
in a motorway café.
For what use your labour with midnight oil,
              blazing trails
into the dark
              climbing 'The Bat'
in stocking soles
              under ghoulish Glencoe moons
  as young Haston did
if no one knows the way you went?

Your puns exploded
– effect without cause –
godawful starshells
that left the night more black.

Those outré traverses
without sinking
one 'deadman' of logic
while you fumbled for a
handhold in the white-out,
      those chunks
      that came
           away
    in your hand,

you jazzman climber trying to build on
your bum notes so they
ain't bum no more,
what use if none can follow you?

In short
I fear if you persist
in leaping direct from peak to peak
like the veritable bloody chamoix,
your audience will tan your hide
and use your poems for

CLEANING THEIR WINDSCREENS

'There was a young lady from France
Who entered a tram in a trance . .'

    the wordman murmured in delirious wonder,
    knocking snow from his boots –
    then hung them in the ingle by their straps,

How can I reply? If words were chocolates,
you'd eat all the hard centres.
But me, I loved Liquid Cherry,
god she was fantastic . .

If I could explain to you the sheer
necessity –
              but then
I'd be rooted in this spot forever
for there's not time
to talk *and* climb
and explanation plods on prosey feet.

    Believe only
that though I aim *per verse ad astra*,
I aim not to be perverse. For me
no other combination will suffice
to unlock the heart on fire,
the mind on ice.

So welcome,
  – pull up your chair –
          welcome to the multi-verse!

(Though it is more sombre since my fall.)

CONFESSIONS OF AN AIRMAN

I do not always come
When I enter the arena at angels twenty,
Thumb wet on the red button –
But it has happened, more than once.

My first kill was an accident.
My second confirmed connections along my nerves.
My third was a mistake – I never meant
To come that close. The eyes were blue, I think.

The rest I put down to shrinking imagination.
My credulity is no longer strained
By ground rolling under my head, this wild
Waltzing, the roar, the shakes,
The cool voices of the girls who guide us –
I have come to accept it all.

This gives me a tighter turn,
A cleaner pair of heels, an extra second
To deliver my metallic telegrams.
And being nearly an ace in this desperate pack,
I merit the best aircraft and fitters, and a wingman
To cover me as I shaft down out of the sun.

All in all, my chances of survival are increasing.

Death is my sudden girlfriend, a wartime romance,
We meet over England several times a day.
As yet I've only brushed her cheek.
Once her lips burned across my thigh.
One of us is not ready to go all the way.

Between meetings I fidget and bitch,
Laugh too loud at her name. I wake sweating,

Seeing again the men she had gone with.
Yet you'll see me stiffen, my eyes brighten,
Each time I rise to meet her again.

THE SOLDIER/BUS TO IZMIR

The soldier has been smoking all night long
But his face is honed with youth, not electricity.
Across this swelter he offers water, and with a wave
At cigarette or uniform or both, regrets his habit.
His battledress is too new, or he too young.
He not comfortable. But resigned. He'll bear with
Being drawn up to his leader's lips, sucked in,
Stubbed out, his ghost regretfully exhaled
Above the maps of battle. He'll go along with this
Dark rattling back to mother. Sweat shinies
His cheekbones. It is a face of unfilled flesh.

We share oranges till the rank
Air sweetens. Shrug, grimace, smile, no more
Is needed. Smoke thickens round his head.
The conductor will always close the window
And we will always open it again.
The moon rises. Night thoughts now
Come static and complete like slides
Shot on a screen. We screw up
Into the mountains. Each moment is lit
From the stub of the last. We move on
Through mountains of ash. We jerk awake
To the smell of oranges. The moon has moved
Or the mountains. His jaw is knife-edge
But his uniform is human-crumpled. Would you like
A smile? Have another. The soldier's nose is hawkbone.
The hills are flat in moonlight. All this scenery
Could be wheeled away, but we don't want to. Our hands
Are occupied with distance, death and cigarettes.
The conductor slams our window shut
And passes round cologne . .

Before dawn he is abruptly asleep.

Slumped back in his seat, mouth open, astonished
By this little death. The last butt drops
From his fingers. I squeeze it out, but cannot sleep
For watching his face flex in the moonlight,
Sweating yet calm as we wind down from the mountains to Izmir.

IN THE TOOL-SHED

'Hummingbirds' he said, and spat. Winged tongues
hovered in the half-light of their names;
cat, cobra, cockatoo rose hissing from the juice.
Piece-time in Africa, amid the terrapins
and jerrycans! Steam swirled above the Congo
of his cup, mangrove-rooted fingers plugged the air –
'Baboons? Make sure you look them in the eyes.' Birds
of paradise! Parrots, paraffin, parakeets
flashed blue and raucous through
thickets of swoe, scythe, riddle, adze.
He sat bow-backed and slack in the dark
heart of his kingdom – creator, guide
in that jungle of sounds, boxes, cloches, canes,
twine, twill, galoshes, jumbled all
across, over, through and into one another
from floor to roof, prowled by fabled carnivores,
the jaguar! the secataurs! Words poke
wet muzzles through reeds of sound
grown enormous overnight. Twin depths
of pitch and pitcher! Elephants lean
patiently upon their ponderous names.
They come in clutches: azaleas, zebras, zambesi.
Orchids, oranges, oran-utangs hang
from their common mouth. Lemming, gorilla, lynx
slink nose to tail through mango groves,
drenched in this sibilant monsoon: moonstone, machettes,
peacocks, paw-paws, lepers, leopards – the walls
are creaking but hold them all, swaying, sweating,
in that dark continent between the ears.
Easy, easy genesis! Old witchdoctor, gardener,
deity of the shed, I grew that garden
from his words, caught the fever
pitch of his Niagara; I follow still
the Orinoco of his blue forearm veins

8

that beat among the talking drums
of all my childhood afternoons.

IN GALLOWAY

In Galloway the drystane dykes that curl
like smoke over the shoulder of the hill
are built with holes
through which sky shows and spindrift birls,
so the wind is baffled but not barred
lest drifting snow smoors a sheltering herd.

There is an art in framing holes
and in the space between the stones.
Structures pared to the bone –
the line that pleases by what's not there
or drydykes laced across the whirling air.

WORDSCAPE: ELEGY FOR ANGUS

Over this cold hearth earth
white birds rise like smoke
settle in ashes
round the plough's long-nailed hand.
Winter hones the east coast's bones
down to a bitter edge:
sharp the wind out of the north
sharp the blades breaking black earth
sharp the winter silhouette of beech and thorn
sharp the heart when coming home.

    *

The voice of this landscape sinks deep
into those who work a lifetime here.
They let fall words like clods.
Darkness circles the country manse,
lochs creak as they freeze.
I walk this wordscape shivering
tracing a sentence ending down an empty road.

    *

For Angus who last summer heard
the death-sentence of the sea
I want the tongue for elegy:

words bared to the bone
words weighted like rocks
split raw from the vein

the poem of stones
built on the edge of a frozen coast
a wall to damn that roar —

11

overhead the long yell of gulls turning inland
as the low sun makes fire of their wings
and the plough digs flames into the winter field.

IT IS THE HEIGHT . . .

It is the height of summer.
The lands are in order.
The King rules.
The Prince is bored.

He sulks indoors, touring the castle
with his entourage mirroring his moods
till he feels himself lost in reflections.
The wind of his will swithers and dies
in the depths of the stagnant afternoons.
Always it is August, his vacation is endless.
In his tower room he debates
the ins and outs
of aimless ennui with two student friends
who will report his condition
to the relevant body . .

The white Queen is in the garden with Uncle,
swaying past the flowers in the shimmering heat.
He whispers in her sails, she laughs and fills.
In hot winds of desire they tack across the lawn . . .

The Councillor's Daughter is down by the river,
entrusting the reeds with her tangled ball
of trivia, waiting on nightfall
when the Prince will unravel her . . .

Imperceptibly, inevitably, and dead on cue,
summer slopes from ripe to rotten.
Wasps crawl from the plums.
The King shrieks from dream to death.

The lands are in disorder.
The King cools.

The Prince is eager in the wings.
At last he has found his vocation.

And now the curtain is rising . . .

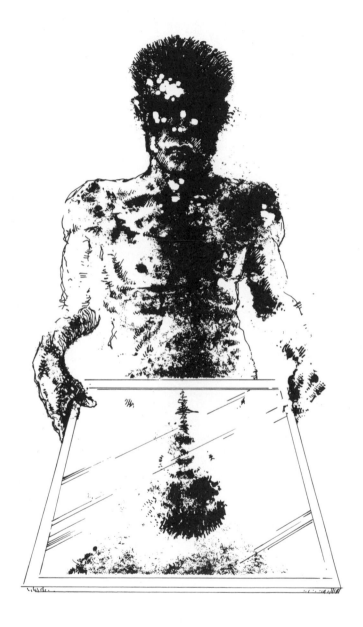

FLAT-MATE

It would have been easier
to share the flat with a mirror.
I wouldn't proffer good mornings
to a reflection and feel them fall away
like a hand no one will shake.
Mirrors can be shut in wardrobes
or draped when they grow tiresome;
they don't follow one from room to room
then outstare the carpet, saying nothing.

In the end I gave up,
left you looking for hours
down the muzzle of the tv screen.

I didn't know you'd go so far
to find someone to talk to.
That night you walked through the mirror
your double took you in his lacerated arms –
cascading blood and glass you both
fell glittering to the floor
and bowed out of this silent flat,
this empty frame.

TIME, OUT FOR THE NIGHT

Time snaps his fingers, orders
the lot. Rare personal appearance
here in the sticks! Our local hotspot
glows as if a draught
now blew on coals. As he sits
between the kitchen and the cabaret,
flowers flare then wilt, cuffs fray, ice
puddles round champagne – replace it all!
Bring on pickles and preserves, anything
in aspic, baked Alaska, the whole gamut
for the great consumer, more glutton
than gourmet – he'd devour
our little place entire
had he somewhere left to sit!
(He still needs clocks to make him tick.)

What commotion, what comingling! Waiters
stutter and rush as candles bloom
then gutter. Pupils contract, flash-lights
expand, collapse like speeded dying suns
as some strive
to get the picture of their lives.
The manager's skull is showing through
(so many old men in charge so long).
Guests are leaving, proposing, giving birth.
Proust dons another overcoat, secures
his autograph. What bowing and scraping
of violins! The music pleases – he nods,
flips a coin that halts the night
till he upturns his curious glass again.

I remember little how my stint was spent,
too busy waiting on his needs to think
or take in the mortal scenery.

Time is up, calls for his cape,
chinks his tip into my ear –
'When cameras click, I stand still,
But it's my ghost you pin up to the wall' –
he leers and leaves, suave racketeer,
lean and youthful in the heart
of his already ageing entourage.

Life seemed to go out of the evening after that.

THE ELEPHANTS

'I liked *The River* but cannot read with pleasure
beyond the lines beginning *Elephants churning the darkness* . . .'
                                        – rejection slip

Elephants! In Anstruther? How you blushed
for those gigantic gate-crashers!
The slender planking of the poem gave way
beneath their scone-like feet. Was it sandalwood joss,
grey cobra uncurling behind the portrait of Baudelaire,
that made the night a broken peach and summoned
those saintly, sweet-toothed vegetarians?
From what dark continent?
Feverish condition of seventeen!
Your pen descended like a whip,
drove them back to limboland.

Ten years on. I lean tonight
on the same sill above a world grown wilder
and – eyes adjusting to the dark – see I
was wrong not trusting my monsters.
That poem began only when they moved in
like thunder grown solid. The rest was scenery.
They alone said something I didn't know –
though they did not speak, their huge heartbeat
was drum enough . . .
                    My ears have aged,
they can't pick up the cry of bats.
But you come to listen in your inner ear,
to hear the shrill whistle of mahoots,
those rapt boys with deft, instinctive thighs
who guide their breasts like a second brain
perched swaying on the first
while on their foreheads brood
those bloody jewels . . . My elephants!

Like shadows round a gloom they are gathering again,
up-river, in fog, in the muzzle of the bridge.
They waver, grow firm, solidify, condense out
of unconscious air, their flanks cross-hatched
and scarred by a thousand lifetimes.
Lightning breaks across their backs
like sticks across the knee.
They cannot go back. I will not send them back.
They alone come unsummoned,
are their own cause, are worth attending to . . .
Dream-beasts of war and burden,
shouldering aside the fog of years
they emerge at last complete,
sensitive, imperishable,
churning the darkness under their feet.

THE DAWN SHIFT

Dawn shifts.
Some make love and others money,
do meditation or the dishes.

Here's one who packs a pipe, makes tea,
takes the path to the shore
not disturbing his contents,

his whole self
the cup he carries
in his writing hand.

     *

The beach shines and sweats.
Already day is filling in
the imprints of dreams.

His place of work is windless.
Here voices are not blown away.
Here he can be reached.

His smoke traces the interior
of an invisible chimney.
Now he is at one with his habit.

     *

Poems if anything are transcriptions of smoke,
the uncoiling world, its precise equipment.
The pipe   the pouch   the cleaners   the knife –

to draw breath without bitterness
the taste of burning must come through

clean   unstale   well understood.

This his work, now the rest
of the day to walk the shoreline
empty and marvellous

the whole sea just filling his cup.

A MAN IS DRIVING

A man is driving on a road that ends
(sure as fate and chance conspire)
in a precipice
(that's life).
But he don't know where
he don't know when
for the road's one long driving round a bend
where what's concealed becomes revealed
only in the moment he's in
and what's revealed becomes concealed
by the continuing turn behind him.

Turn any corner at any time of any day
and the trail may end
in the dream-fall
where you never wake
because this time you hit bottom –
this is the code of the road we groove on
as day and night on the jewelled carriageway
wheel and white line kiss and part and kiss again.

I do not live in dread or in anticipation.
I do not drive faster or slower.
I do not choose my way or means
of transport to offer my neighbours
pleasing reflections of themselves.
Whatever highway we unroll tonight,
whoever's passenger I am,
the cat's eyes come alive as I pass by
and stare into me, unwinking and calm.
As out of the dark they swing
and back into the dark they fade,
I am not afraid
for we are a-travellin' light

and we spark in the moment we're in.

WE HAVE COME AT LAST...

from the French of *Dominique le Roux*

We have come at last to the island
of Patmos. Why should we persist
in trying to trap
the wind in a box? Here, clouds
do not hold back the sky, the shadows
that sweep the abandoned cave
don't stir up dust or visions.
There is jubilation in those voices
that ring and fade gladly
without conch-shells or legends
to echo them on.

There is no need to grasp
what we hold now.

The shape of statues,
even their whiteness,
no longer interests us.
To what end should we imitate
anything at all? We are born
of the onrush that brings us here
to this beach of shells like
abandoned ears. The kingdom is at hand;
we need not stoop to pick it up
to hear the sea
cupped in the murmur of our blood.

PORTOBELLO BEACH
An Off-Season Entertainment

The Café

We took a window-seat,
surveyed the place. A coffee-house
in its post-Johnsonian phase. A shrine
to angular veneer worn thin
according to the fashion – Art Deco
at the third remove. A sunburst mirror
flicked morning me back into my eyes;
with affection and despair I recognize
the tawdry self and its surroundings.

We count the false fronts
from formica to paint-on chrome
to the spray that glues the bee-hive
honey-tinted dome of Our Lady
Of The Counter, drowsing in the smoke
of her morning cigarette.
No movement, voice or draught disturbs
that spiral fade up to the ceiling.
It is as if, in this backwater,
life's rope has finally untwisted to
each seperate strand and left her slack-
handed and alone, curled back against the wall.
All things have found their level
in that emblematic slouch. A great tide
has gone out round her keeled-over head.
The final peace perhaps, the world unwound . . .

 Can one find Fresh Gateau here?
 (She smiled, and then outside
 the watery sun was wasting its light.)

I did once, though it seemed
beyond my means, being but a blue
jean-filling teenager. My
café-society days! When this green
and yellow paint was blazing new
as Rock n' Roll and Pepsi-Cola,
we'd smoke straws, cinnamon, nicotine, hash,
anything that was brash and masterful
in the glow of the Rockola.
We parked our bikes to its beat,
strolled in, pumped tanners in the slot
bought swagger-time to sit
reclining in the shadow of its shout . .
                    Sheer boredom
on fire at the edges.
The Great Pretenders put a match
to the trash crumpled in our ash-tray
and watched the flames lick in
towards the centre . . .

Here's Action!
By the door (whose stippled glass
yields neither view nor image of ourselves
four malcontents as befits their age
are putting the boot
in a desultory way
into a Guess-Your-Weight machine –

          Heavy!
        Yes, this must
      be Scotland, the half-cut
    ragged fingernail
on the outflung arm of Europe:
my hang-out, my country,
my song, my shanty
east-coast town, last resort
of the terminally out-of-season.

(But you, you'd flourish anywhere,
running barefoot down the tenement stair
to greet me though I was late.
I felt then the fist of my will
fit the glove of my fate.
It is sudden hope like a blow
from nowhere that brings us
winded to Portobello.)

*   *   *

The Complaint
(waiting for Cake)

We placed our order
and while we waited, each palmed
a circle in the steamy glass
and peered out through those portholes . . .

    The walls of Dreamland are split and warped
    and we can see into the late Fun Fair.
    The Kosmic Wheel has ceased to spin;
    rusting chairs creak in the wind,
    poised always at the same
    point of fortune. Deserted now
    the Shooting Gallery with those grinning
    tin targets we never could quite shoot down.
    The sights were set high. The Ghost Train
    don't scare, the Hall of Mirrors
    can't raise a laugh now that distortion rules.
    No longer does the organ stir
    dancers like soup in the pot
    round the mezzazine floor, beneath
    the simple magic of the spinning globe.
    Even the musak has piped down. Life

has gone out to lunch
in California maybe
– though that's debatable –
and is not expected back
this century.

Me, I'm moved to affection and despair
at this café, this self, this Scotland.
An aged relative, wheedling, cantankerous,
playing on our nerves and sympathy
as she sprawls on the crumpled bed
of the North Sea. Talking always
of the past. The golden age,
the forced marriage, the lost
ungrateful children . . . An endless litany
of blood-betrayals on quartz-
glittering heights, rumbles in back-alleys,
the secret thrust and gasp against the wall.
You cling on and on, that we might never
eat our cake and leave fulfilled
but hesitate here, swung back
on two legs of a chair.

    – How can we ever leave?

– How can we ever stay?

*   *   *

Interlude

I watch her lips kiss coffee froth,
Her neat mouth close round cake;
Each movement stirs inside me
An unlocated ache.

Such gusts of tenderness and lust
Make me avert my eyes;
She's lit beneath the skin as if
Flesh were a thin disguise.

For what? Inside her body's mesh
There's something seems to glow;
There is a love which burns to ash
All that we used to know.

I watch her lips kiss coffee-froth,
Her neat mouth eat gateau . . .

*   *   *

The Exit

This egg-stain is immovable.
The mushroom cloud above the expresso
has become part of the furniture.
The very air's congealed. Sauce, vinegar,
sun, all watered-down. This ash-tray
overflows with snuffed-out buts.
Clichés like tartan cellophane
wrap up everything we feel and touch.

The last consumers order wildly.
The hot and wet has taken on
the wrinkled skin of age.
We are lovers; this is a fluke
like hitting jackpot on that
one-armed bandit in the corner.
Never bank on it . . .

This is a café we internalize
and carry with us all our days.
A moveable feast! We must push
the same door open again and again
into the world we borrow,
accept today and will tomorrow
or sit here in the gloom forever
and never get our gateau.
We have paid, so
let us go now, you and I . . .

   The Gateau was delicious
   in its own special way,
   She remarked. Life is not
   a bowl of cherries – but then
   it's not a bowl of anything;
   being not hollow inside,
   having no outside rim.

      Then we rose and left the old café
      of that winter seaside town.

      We can be zeroes, just for one day.

TWO

THAT NIGHT

That night we met
crashed more like
bodywork flew and

we fused and screwed
wham through a hedge
finished on the edge

after we lay still
critical condition
the moonlight bled
across her forearm

our headlights skewing
out into deepest space
where energies collide
making each other anew

LAST NIGHT'S POEM . . .

Last night's poem viewed today
still looks, to my surprise . . . okay.
A little dishevelled,
but this posture of innocence
would be lost in correction
and the dark commas that curl
across her fluent face
redeem in charm what they lack in precision.

Last night it seemed she was
a single quote from perfection.
Her cry omitted nothing
as she came to the pure thing she could be
and in return her knowledge rose in me . . .

Last night's poem viewed today
lies spread out on the sheet.
No longer divine, but good just the same.
As I watch, she wakes, scans me thoughtfully,
then claims me by my name.

WATCH

He kept his watch on when he slept
in that white room where
the ceiling poised to blot
the sweating error on the sheet below –

it strapped up more than his wrist.
When he woke – black afraid –
groping in the shadow of his shout,
a gesture would pull that little moon
before his eyes, made space,
pushed sky back up again.

Now he does not need
that soft tether round his dreams.
It lies loose on the cabinet,
quiet as a pulse.
There is a new watch
in the sleeping face beside him;
any time in the night
the hand across his chest recalls
the place this is, the time that was.

MELISSA

Straight from the water
the camera caught her
moving from light into shade.

I pin the photo to the wall.
Time knifes us from behind
aiming for the heart –

we can't believe it
we double-take in arthritic surprise
we drag ourselves into the shade:

coughing up the years we lie
flicking through stills
calling for water.

JOURNAL OF THE FIRST WINTER

This winter is total.

First frost found us erecting fences,
second stripped our nerves to wire.
Blizzards piled up, set hard
in night-long silences.
It soon became impossible to walk out.
We have retreated inside,
eke out what remains:
with little appetite or talk
we make love without heat.

Windows remain opaque.

> *

Living here on the frontier
something had to give
when we cannot.

An unwritten contract
is being shredded
into millions of pieces,

they are falling quietly
behind my eyes.

We sit here
in helpless peace
while the sky gives way.

> *

Snow is still falling,
it is rain made slow.

A sinking feeling
made evident
as a hand falls away . . .

We burnt our summer's wood,
photos, letters, everything
in one last blazing night . . .

Mountains of ash
in the grate. Block the chimney
before something comes in or escapes.

    *

Pain is white. It blanks out
every other feature.

When she took to her bed
I forgot myself in waiting on her.
She would swither in fever,
restless with muttered inner worlds
where she thawed in the arms
of men from the South,
then lie still for days –

eyes obscure
under the pale drift of her hair.

    *

We have held out. There is
a trickling outside our door.
Soon she will be able to walk.

For the first time in months
I am unprepared. Ice is
simpler than water.
Everything will shift again,
unpredictably, downhill.

In our dreams tonight
the barbs on the fences
begin to bud . . .

So ends our first winter.

PROSTHETICS

I am a man mocked by a phantom limb
that hurts like hell. Months later
it fools me still – coming home
I anticipate warm rooms and cooking
then stumble over a cold threshold.
Entering each room handfirst
I feel for light.

In time illusion, like the excuse it is,
will wear thin through repetition.
I will fall for it
no more. Standing on my own one leg
I shall hop around for a replacement
that will look nearly natural,
that will fit near as damn me,
who at the end of the day
I can always detach.

These days I am learning to whistle
to accompany my rolling gait;
life's little amputations
give us a nautical air.

THE GLOVE

This room need not speak of her.
It is enough
the air is hard to breathe.

On the table, a flattened glove.
Nothing has moved
since she slipped out.

There is no calling from kitchen or shore.

It is the absence
of a hand
touching us –

no one dares
touch anything at all.

    *

Dust haunts
that place the eyes avoid.

For this ghost,
exorcism exists:

in time
rooms will be aired
furniture shifted
old echoes interrupted
by a young voice –

you will not notice
the glove is gone

never know who threw it out

to the end
its splay fingers
grasp nothing.

PATIENCE

The courts of conscience have adjourned.
In the park, leaves edge the air
with fire as they fall discarded.
He sits up late, playing patience –

a deck of memories
that won't come clean.
The pattern is always incomplete,
the ending different but the same.

He shuffles through the pack again
unable to discard her image,
between his fingers the season burns
unattended to a tail of ash –

he flicks it off without a second thought,
deals the deck again but cannot let it drop.

BY THE POOL

Tell the truth
through my indian summer
she was cordially mine.

Green and sharp
her youth hit a dry spot
on a tongue tired of wagging.

Her fruitful sway
worth sweating for.
One swallow made that summer.

Now I sit in the shade
in a panama hat
sipping on memories –

at the end of everything
the exact taste of her
lingering between the teeth.

TOWARDS A MIRAGE
(from the French of Francois D'Alançon)

Setting out

She has seen worlds pass
No need to put out
her sometimes tendered body

Generations bring
the restless winds

She is wearing slowly down to sand
returning to the sea

You travel towards her
when you cup water
transparent in your hands

Cambridge

Surely the river runs more clearly here today
You are rediscovering the red city
restoring the fields

Through fields and cloisters
you have come this far –
bridge over the Isis

Years slip down your throat
as you drink
thinking of the future

The White One

Hydra they built you on the sea's flank
headlands and gardens
arteries coiled into stone

the white one
lashed to the top of the cliff

Mouth suckled by summer
lips still full of night
men trickle through her fingers

Now the boats are out
her belly carries only
brackish water . . .

When she crumples
into dust and tears
beautiful and susceptible as ever

they will make clay
and fashion it
in her image again

In Gardhaia

Rest by the well in Gardhaia

The day gives birth to
houses seamed with stone
walls packed tight
around the market place

Higher up the ladder of light
between the ochre and the blue
the place of Allah
the mystery of ramparts

where a woman held her body
against the stone
embracing
outfacing the invader

We have no entry here
Our thirst makes wine of water
We drink but we do not understand
this well of blue light in Gardhaia

Dar el Beida

On oiled blue bearings
clouds slide back
the hatches of night –

a bow wave of light
breaking round the boats at Dar el Beida

Legend of Bahadja

She would initiate them
in the joy of perfumes
ambered scents explored on
the mosaic
beside smoking pools
in the shadow of the hammam

Legend of Bahadja
the joyful one
For a long time now
women have been veiled
children have been playing
only in dirty streets

the eyes of Allah
look down
the soldiers' guns

The Embrace

On Erg
silence glints
sieved clean by wind

Imperceptible migration
of each grain
on the shoulder of the dune

At last the mirage is recognized
One and the same
when all is broken down –

the salt grains glittering on her arm
the dunes encircling
vestiges of an old sea

The Point Of Departure

The dogs have been barking
all night long
The muezzin fell silent in vain

We must leave her
this exhausted city
stretched out dreaming
hips half-buried in sand
fingers trailing in the bay

Perhaps we did not love
the desert enough
the rose of the dunes
the dust of the roads
her shifting veils

One might think a journey
stains only our clothes
but our eyes are different now

staring at those flowers
that seed and wither in a day
along the ditch that irrigates
the fields and city
of her birth

THREE

THE PIPER'S REPLY

Let there be plain speech between us.
I cannot rid your town of rats.

You seem surprised. Panic scuttles
behind broad waistcoats.
I cannot sanitize this crooked town,
contagion rises from hand to hand
like money
             to the houses on the hill.
There is no keeping it
in quarantine with whore and cripple.

One cannot erect barriers with songs.
What squeals in dreams
gnaws through to daylight.
It should be clear
if you employ me
I play only to myself –
no rest
             from my own vermin.
The moment I perfect a tune
they grow bored and multiply . . .

    Cash for journeying
    bread for belly
    wine down throat
    tenderness to ease
    the isolation of skin

    my needs are not original

    What cities I have seen
    what plagues
    they seem stitched together

along one seam
black barge and its reflection . . .

I will not steal your children.
If some leave
                    that music beats
inside their drum, not mine.
The one who does not return
limped here in any case.

This pipe
                    tugs me forward.
I cannot aid your pestilence.
Yet if your rats ressemble mine
you may gain relief
as I pass by

piping to keep my spirits up
before I go under the hill.

SHADOWED

Someone somewhere is watching me.
No guardian angel nor the lord god almighty
not from the CIA
not my mother or father or analyst.

Not my death deciding when
best to interrupt
not even my conscience –
he makes no judgements.

He eludes all options.
Such is his nature or lack of it.

    *

He is always the peripheral
edge of vision
just across the street
as I go about my business
checking the change I'm handed,
collar up, hat down, a scarf of smoke
where his face must be –
a lonesome cliché no one will bring in from the rain.

Under the brightest sun he shadows me
after midnight he is there
curled up in the corner
a crumpled question mark.

    *

The old judge has bowed out
and will not be back.
Without a god one still conjures
a hollow man across the road, a guy
who sees one as one is
who is never deceived or impressed
who simply watches

a sounding board
an empty overcoat.

EXILES

We have lived thousands of years
in the kingdom of longing.
There are no free citizens here.

Even the ascetics
are bound to the next rung
on their ladder of light.

For us, each week
six leaden cylinders discharge;
on the seventh day, the hammer
clicks on empty.

Tommorow, we say, we will
be home, eating holy bread –
our words dig deep pits
to starve or be sick in.

THE HARE IN WINTER (from Aragon)

If the universe ressembles a barracks
from whatever city I sleep in tonight,
if miles away the stranger fishes our lochs
and draws forth our riches with money and dynamite,

I am no longer at home even in my heart.
Is this my generation or even my country
when I fear your riches as much as your poverty,
knowing they will take advantage of both?

Now we live like the hare in winter
turning neutral and vanishing against the snow.
Unnoticed we must survive the killing season
until the emigrants look back again,

their eyes like arrows,
their faces taut as bows.
A generation is standing on the shore,
waiting for an omen as a fleet waits for the wind.

We read the entrails.
We gather in the stadium.
We stare to the bottom of our glasses
trying to see beyond the next round –

here on the gallows-arm of Europe
we need a sign that we might hope again.
Our dreams run deep in us. Once roused
we will not sleep again this side of sanity.

THE CRACK

(i)   Accounts vary as to when the Crack appeared

        Last night last week last century
        you looked up from the daily news
        glanced round on your way home
        saw it in your lover's eyes those cracked despairing eyes
        spilling water unable to bear any longer
        the world in their blue vase
        and there it was
        evident as sky itself
        and as with those sudden certainties –
        someone's staring at you your phone is tapped
        love has run through your fingers again –
        you realise things have been that way
        for some while and feeling foolish and very much
        behind the times you curse you rise you make for the door

        You need only look down
        into the puddle of self or anyone
        to see it reflected there   the collapse   the break
        that final vivid Crack across the sky

(ii)   Impossible! they said   not the sky
        not our everloving ceiling

                        cracked!
        We may have punched a few holes
        but everything can be repaired   we have
        our sticky patches
                 These doomsters
        are bad news   they do not graduate
        from our fiction shelves they have no place
        in our projections

                              Sky   like us   is held up
by tension   each half leaning on
the other
                    sky tolerates
the shattering
when we clap our hands
this is our theatre   we play
as we please
                    Not on our heads
these white pillars this blue roof

O not our everlasting sky   Is blue!   Is sound!

(iii)   Everyone who could see did see
        at some time or other what had happened
        but most being human and thus
        capable of denying thrice the obvious
        not wanting to spoil the picnic
        went on kissing and killing and flying their kites

        Of those who saw the lightning and couldn't forget
        some took shelter some felt sick
        went indoors and covered their eyes
        some took to the bottle some stuffed therein
        messages to whoever however unlikely came after
        some went about their business as before living
        a little harder a little more honest
        jealous of their time counting on thunder

        Then the shock-wave hit
        the sky fell in and yes
        that was it

A NIGHT JOURNEY

i) the descent

A night journey is being made though you
do not know it at the time
that time without
faith or dignity   stripped even
of fingerprints   shuffling
into this hovel
            this desert
                this winter
                    this night
                        you go
down into the dark
world under this one
into the belly
of a whale of a time
into the hollow hill we heap
            around ourselves
            to feel
                    invisible
            lying with the dead
            in their dissenting passages

            where we may hide
            from the unspeakable
            that is to say
            ourself

As piping grows muffled
then fades out
like something not worth remembering

one is alone with the sword
                    the staff
                the book
            the fiddle
        whatever hangs shattered at one's side

and a faithful companion
who may be man woman hound it does not matter
in any case they are dumb

as you walk into the sea into the sun
staring down its muzzle
                        pressed flat
                    body-black
                mere silhouette
            limned by fire

            one has become
        a forked stick
        the notch
one sights along in murderous moments

ii) the return

    We went down
as necessary
hating it
into the heart of
sun darkness hovel hill
in any case the heart —

not all return   those who do not die enough
are not reborn   those who do not stumble
will never dance   those who do not gutter out
do not illuminate   find the pavement a tightrope
and walk it   that is to say
live –
      All this
   that we might
   be thrown up
   spewed forth
   like something indigestable

      into a new kingdom
      unrolled on familiar shores
            The legendary self

      walking back
from the sea from the sun
the pipe   the staff   the sword   the book
whatever instrument made whole again
the companion speaking now
powered by fusion
inexhaustable

the door creaks open
into this dawn
clear-headed
with light footfall and taut
harmonious string

    nameless
      weightless
        glowing like coal

      the fiddler now steps to the road

DISSENTING PASSAGES
a fugitive diary

    My friends,
those too brave or slow to go underground
those whose condition was critical
were brought in overnight –

dawn
folded back
over empty beds.

An arresting opening?
An old story. At present
I am losing myself
in the deceptive country of my childhood.
My profile is low my nose is in the mud my mind
well that is in the mud too –

I scream
on paper only
not so loud or satisfying

but the echo need never fade.
The poets of my youth would enduce madness
real or feigned to enliven themselves.
Luxury! I am as sane
as necessary. In this ambiguous country
I am making myself
                        scarce

     *   *   *

Whatever form the search took I became
the shape it couldn't contain –
paper to stone,
dandruff to comb.

As ever I define myself
in opposition.

*   *   *

For the first month I lay flaked out
at the roots of a wavering hedge
while recruits combed the fields
in white camouflage jackets.
In their skillful palms I see
the glint of razors,
my demon barbers
come to trim me down.

    The hounds stop
    inches from my skull
    my fate spins
    in the sworl of their saliva –

they swing away
on paths I cannot trace nor want to.
It seems I have already
ceased to smell human.

*   *   *

Running away from feeling only to run
into someone running the other way

we bruise easily
we apologize
we do not become intimate
we do not show hard feelings

we part
each running the other way . . .

*   *   *

Nurses have ringed the moors.
They have read my file, seen surrender to women
comes more easily to me.
Loudspeakers hail. Apparently
my state of mind lacks

    frontiers
    a consensus   a constitution
    means of defence   an economy
    an anthem   a flag   I may wave
    a white hankerchief
    I am its sole citizen
    this is called madness

    (fidelity is low
    the prerecorded tape
    whines negative feedback
    its impulses lie too close
    to the source of power
    the system is near
    overloading)

They claim better a flat in town
than castles in the air
one can sustain anything but doubt
I must commit myself
back into the box
jack . . .

But their offers of bosom
comfort and care
are distorted by the technology
that bears them.
The wind shreds their pleas.
Spasms of sniggering
jerk through me like shivers.
They leave . . .
                    They leave food in baskets,
some of their best dogs have eaten it
and in their deaths convulse
like the last Beatgroups.

    Thus the raised fist
    obscures its target.
    This is its only limiting factor.

*   *   *

I am ringed around by voices
that sound out the hole
I inhabit and am. Threading
through ears, words tug the brain
this way and that. In their cradle
I am the invisible cat,
fighting to reappear
behind this fugitive grin.

    *   *   *

Hounds howl in the throat
of night   the Hunter is mid-leap
across the northern sky   his belt
studded with scalps
that spark like crazy   the year
shrinks deeper dark

I am wheeling toward the river   seeking
blessed confusion of scent
to shake from my heels
the baying of thought
the crude stars
that stalk above our solitude

*   *   *

The refuge was surrounded
at halflight, the keys
based on impressions
of the fugitive that was.
They probed the weak spot,
felt something click
in those dark passages,
pushed and found –

the door firm,
the lock intractable.

For those who come
armed with the past
the stable is always bare. The trap
door mimes their open mouths
when they crash in –

empty cradle
pressed in shining, already cooling, straw.

I lie awake
in the black country
monitoring the broken sleep,
the scuffles, snores, outcries
of my fellow creatures.
At the pad of our predators
we shrink towards vanishing point.
Who has not heard the rustle of their skirts,
the approach of invisible instruments
as the nightnurses descend?
We hear a shriek, a rattle
as curtains are drawn
round one of our number.
We cower in silence. We burrow
deeper. We wait for dawn.
We do not break cover.

*   *   *

It is a fugitive code
the only one he knows –

*Do not enter box
until exit is clear.*

The road is dark
on the way from somewhere
to somewhere –

we are fighting for
the right of passage.

*   *   *

Yet there are compensations.
Hunger generates visions of food
finer than anything held in the fist.
Great thirst alone
turns water into wine.

In the desert
I have performed miracles.
I sleep. I wake. I move about
the surface of the earth.
I have talked with the dead, been
unspeakably tender with old loves.
In their absence
I have explained everything to everyone.

In this sand-polished silence,
complete speech.

In the desert
we need mirages,
shimmerings held
in the blue back of the mind.
We may never see their originals;
it is enough to know they exist
somewhere, on the other side of the world,
to keep us gasping towards bright palms.

I am well attended.
At night the moon is shining
or it is not. Each has its uses.
Never has the sun
risen so uniquely for me . . .

This dawn is not my enemy's.

*   *   *

I have grown thin as my nerves.
Daylight is too bright. My memory
is a jumble of presents.

I wrap and unwrap them over and over.

Such inappropriate responses! Fury
when a bootlace breaks. Indifferent
as bayonets needle the stack I'm in.
Shuddering when a ptarmigan
– winter plumage almost complete –
whirrs up from my feet.

I wrap
my greatcoat round myself and myself
round the spark I nurse.

Next to nothing,
  a simple point,
I balance on the needle of solitude.

*   *   *

I stumble into her ditch one night
too weary to mutter 'My mistake'
and crawl back out. We whisper through the night,
our voices rusted and strange. She smells
of woodsmoke, her skin is pale
                              hard as birch.

She replies
        I smell
like a fresh grave
and might have stopped for a toothbrush
but may she crawl
under my greatcoat?

With some difficulty I unbutton.

*   *   *

The sky at dawn is hungover,
haggard, bloodshot at the rim. I find
we have crept under one skin.
There is no wind
like the draught blowing in
from someone else's world.

I murmur
    this pillar of steam
    will expose our position.
She replies
    survival at any price
    is a blank cheque
    without a signature –

    worth
    damn all.

There are times when all we need
is a touch on the arm
before we sleep.

*   *   *

It was too dangerous. We could not
disentangle in emergency.
We were two mirrors set face to face.

We parted while still able
to walk unaided.
She took some fabric from my coat
and made good the lack
with something from her own
(these other patches
are the result of common wear,
they have no healing properties).

When memory has its christmases
I unwrap her night after night
and stare into her pale frame searching myself.

*   *   *

Tonight snow is falling. As I kneel
behind the wall, a crown settles
then vanishes upon my head.

I am feeling
a way towards another kingdom.

Revelations drift onto open palms.
They cannot last they cannot lie.
This secret passage is almost complete.

*   *   *

I have been declared
                              'Officially Lost'.
The search-light is turned off
I am in
the utter dark.
Dissent defined me it was
a security of sorts.

No is not so hard an answer.

Now I have become
a danger to myself.
Must hunt for if necessary strike
a match in the night
a tiny Yes
or give myself up –

this urge
the same one
that tugs this cigarette to my lips
grinds sparks out under my heel.

*   *   *

I am standing in the dark
across the road from the old university
I am listening to the soldiers sing
in their new billet

They are my kind
solid and familiar
I long to shed
the greatcoat of night
and step humbly into that warm, lit room . . .

   My friends,
I hesitate
shifting in my mud-encrusted shoes.

*   *   *

WE SPOKE OF FALLING

We spoke of falling
into despair
as if it were a well.

It was much bigger than that.

We did not drown
in that dead sea;
on the shore we saw
glittering bodies
lick salt crystals
from each other's wounds . . .

Now we are bound
to thirst –
no well in the world
can slake this tenderness.